The Root Chakra Solution

Belinda Broome

Published by Ampersand Rue Incorporated, 2020.

While every precaution has been taken in the preparation of this book, the publisher assumes no responsibility for errors or omissions, or for damages resulting from the use of the information contained herein.

THE ROOT CHAKRA SOLUTION

First edition. February 18, 2020.

Copyright © 2020 Belinda Broome.

Written by Belinda Broome.

Introduction

I stood on an unnaturally sunny New York City street, blinking, stunned. I held a box with framed pictures of my kids, a mug and assorted stuff I'd used to make my desk feel like a slice of home in the office ten stories above the spot where I now stood. My mood did not match the sunny day. Duane Reade bags hung from my arms, filled with gym clothes and the surprising amount of stuff I'd managed to gather in the six months I'd been working in this place. Six months that had ended just a few minutes before, with a scene straight out of the movie *Up In The Air*: a packet, an all-business firing. The job had seemed promising, a new division in an established company, my favorite kind of place. It had been a chance to build something new at a time I really needed it. But that chance had just ended. I'd been unceremoniously fired and given time to gather my things. Now here I was, in the incongruously cheery sunshine, blindsided. The division just hadn't worked out and they'd let most of us go. I was newly divorced and in over my head on a mortgage I couldn't afford. Now, I was out of a job.

Some spidey sense I'd had most of my life but which I didn't listen to nearly enough had told me to drive into work that morning instead of taking the smog-coughing bus I normally took. If you've never driven into New York during rush hour, you may not know that this was a pretty unusual move to make based on a spidey sense. Traffic can be brutal, the toll is insane and parking costs a chunk you should probably put aside for your kids' college tuition. But having my car nearby proved handy as I lugged all the worldly possessions I'd collected as I tried to make this new job feel like home. I got my car and dumped the stuff in the back. It was only then I remembered I'd made a coffee date with a friend in the suburban town I lived in about ten miles outside of New York City. I was supposed to work from home that day, and on days I worked from home it helped to schedule some human contact. I had been called into the office (I now understood why) and had forgotten to cancel the date.

I just wanted to go home and curl up into a ball until it was time to go pick my kids up from elementary school. But something told me to keep the coffee date. When I got there, my friend could tell immediately that there was something wrong. I told her, even though my instinct is usually to keep bad news to myself in a mix of shame and desire for privacy.

"Do you want me to do Reiki on you?" she asked.

I knew what Reiki was, an energy healing technique that involves moving hands near a person, but I had no idea this friend of mine did it. She'd just taken a course, she explained. I wasn't sure what it would do, but the idea of someone caring enough about me to want to help me heal felt good. So I agreed.

She began to move her hands near me. I couldn't tell you what, exactly, she did. All I know is that I felt an intense whoosh, a sense of something rushing through me as if I was hollow and water was moving through me as if out a spigot. The emotions were intense. She said, "It's okay to let go."

All the emotions swirled through me: the fear of how I would support myself and my kids. The shame of being found wanting, even though intellectually I understood I had done nothing wrong. The overwhelm of what I would have to do next: a job search, maybe even selling my house. The apprehension of what to tell my kids. I cried like I can't remember having cried before. When I was done, it was as if all the grief of being fired, all the fear, all the things I'd been trying to clench inside had just drained out of me. I was clear and felt strong.

Whatever this was, I knew I needed more.

Right around that time, I discovered an online quiz that determined the state of a person's chakras. It was a simple test: answer some questions, and out came the results. My throat chakra was overactive, a fact that almost made me giggle. I'd never had any challenge speaking my mind, maybe sometimes to my detriment. My crown chakra was open, which felt right. I felt a strong connection to the divine. My root chakra, however, that indicator of how safe I felt in the world, was the most underactive of all. An underactive root chakra means you are closed off from all the things that sustain you, and it often manifests in feelings of lack of safety, in money problems, and in unexpected shocks like the one I'd just suffered. There are many reasons for this condition, which we'll cover in this book. Best of all, there are many things you can do to change it.

I embarked on a mission to figure out what I could do about it. I consulted experts, I read books, I scoured the web endlessly. Little by little, I tried things. The results were remarkable. From the moment of being that woman, blinking away tears on a New York City street, I went on to craft a life of fulfillment, of safety, of joy, and great independence and financial security. What follows on these pages is everything I learned on the journey and a step-by-step plan of how you can do the same.

We can't help the things that have led to our feelings of lack of safety or our unhealthy relationship with money. They are rooted in childhood, and sometimes are even ancestral. If you were raised around lack, or with instability, this takes its toll on your psyche and your root chakra. But you are not powerless. You can open your root chakra. You can let in more abundance than you even imagine possible right now. You can live the life of your dreams.

Your root chakra is the base of your well-being, your physical health, your sense of belonging in this world. If it's closed off, or underactive, it can lead to energy imbalances that touch every area of your life. When it's overactive it can cause issues too. (We'll cover that as well). When you work to make your root chakra balanced, open and vibrant, the results will be fast, and they'll be amazing.

Are you ready? Let's go.

Is your root chakra underactive? Answer these questions.

Since the root chakra governs your sense of safety, abundance, and your connection to the physical world, a few simple questions will help you discern whether you need to work to open it further.

Would you consider yourself an anxious person?

Are you an "overthinker"?

Do you have trouble focusing sometimes?

Do you live paycheck to paycheck?

Do you feel like you don't fit in?

Do you struggle with having enough energy?

Are you "sure" bad things will happen?

Do you often feel like you can't afford to do the things you want to do?

Do you keep yourself from doing fun things with your friends or treating yourself because you can't afford it?

Do you feel hopeless about ever fixing your financial situation?

On the flip side, are you drawn to fanciful ways of making money, like entering online sweepstakes or finding "get rich quick" schemes?

Do you spend time imagining the possible bad outcomes to things?

Do you have digestive issues, hemorrhoids, or autoimmune issues?

Did you grow up with parents or caregivers who often told you "we can't afford that"?

Do you remember having to "go without" as a child?

Were you called a dreamer growing up?

Are you often "in your head," or do you feel like you're not living in the moment?

IF YOU ANSWERED "YES" to more than four of these questions, you could use doing some work on your root chakra. If you answered "yes" to seven or more, you will benefit immensely from the tools and exercises in this book. Practiced regularly and with self-love, the exercises in this book can lead to a joyful, easy, abundant life. Give yourself the gift of opening your root chakra and watch the magical changes in your life.

One note about this work: some of the suggestions in this book involve addressing health issues. Obviously, this is not a book by a medical professional and is not intended to diagnose or treat any health issue. As always, before changing your diet, taking any supplements, or starting or modifying an exercise regimen, talk to your doctor and other health professionals. Medical issues are real and should be addressed promptly. Take care of you. That's part of healing your root chakra too.

1. What are Chakras? A primer

So what exactly are chakras? If we can't see them or touch them, how do we know they are there? Chakra, in Sanksrit, means "wheel" or "disk." Many spiritual traditions have identified the energy field of the body, and although we can't see it, tuning in can lead you to feel it. For now, it's okay if you're not quite sure what they are, or how they feel. Just understanding the basics is enough to get you started. And what I like to say to skeptics is: even if you have no tangible evidence of this, and it's just working on a purely psychological level, who cares, if it works? To be clear, root chakra work can be powerful and profound. I'm just suggesting that if you have questions, or feel unsure, it's okay to put those aside and do the work anyway. The comprehension and the "knowing" will come with time. It's okay to not have all the answers right now.

The chakra system begins at the base of your spine. This is where your root chakra is located. It is within your body, but also extends outside it, as a red, slowly spinning wheel we call the root chakra. The root chakra is where all energy flows into you, so if it is cloudy or blocked, your entire chakra system will be out of whack.

The **root chakra** corresponds to your connection to your body, to the Earth.

Its color is red.

Its location is at the base of your spine.

Its qualities include: it connects to your feelings of safety and belonging. It informs how safe you feel and guides your financial life. It rules all things earthy, like how strong and connected to your body you feel. Have you ever felt "spaced out" or "all in your head"? That's a root chakra dysfunction. An underactive root chakra can lead to difficulties connecting with family and loved ones, a feeling of lack of control, as well as anxiety and money problems.

The root chakra is often seen as a red, spinning wheel, a rich and beautiful ruby-red jewel tone. When you first start to do this work, it may be spinning sluggishly, or have dark patches on it (imagine dust on a filter). Any time you visualize it, imagine a clear, bright, rich red, and if you notice any spots, send light to them until your whole root chakra is glowing a vibrant red. Don't worry if this feels hard, or if you don't visualize anything at first. Everyone's method of doing this work is different, and there is no wrong way. There is a chapter on visualization later in this book. If you enjoy visualizing, then that chapter holds several techniques for you. But if you don't, not to worry. There are plenty of other techniques you can try.

The **sacral chakra** corresponds to your connection to pleasure and creativity

Its color is orange

Its location is approximately four fingers below the navel

Its qualities include: it's tied to your reproductive and sexual organs. It informs how fluid, creative and alive you feel, how able you are to give and receive pleasure. Have you ever been hard on yourself, guilty, or felt out of balance? That's an underactive sacral chakra.

The **solar plexus chakra** corresponds to your sense of self

Its color is yellow

Its location is between the navel and the bottom of the rib cage

Its qualities include: it's connected to your sense of self and accomplishment. It informs how competent, worthy and effective you feel. Have you ever felt a lack of self-esteem, an ongoing overabundance of anger, or a crippling perfectionism? Do you struggle with depression, digestive issues, diabetes or liver issues? These are solar plexus chakra issues. (As always, consult a trained medical professional for health issues).

The **heart chakra** corresponds to your love of self and others

Its color is green

Its location is in the center of your chest, in the heart region

Its qualities include: it's connected to your emotions of love for yourself and others, for your ability to trust and feel loved your attachments and how compassionate and understanding you are. Have you ever felt a lack of trust, jealousy, moodiness, and pessimism? Those are heart chakra issues.

The **throat chakra** corresponds to your ability to make yourself heard

Its color is bright blue

Its location is at the base of your throat

Its qualities include: it's connected to your ability to communicate, to speak your mind, to stand up for yourself and be an advocate for yourself and others. Have you ever felt timid, afraid to speak up, like no one was listening, or like you couldn't get your point across? Do you have issues offering constructive criticism or do you intend to take up artistic endeavors but something always stands in your way? Are you afraid of public speaking? These are throat chakra issues.

The **third eye chakra** corresponds to your ability to see things as they are

Its color is indigo blue

Its location is between your eyebrows

Its qualities include: it's connected to your ability to see clearly, and that's not just physical vision. It's related to intuition (that "I feel it in my bones" feeling), insight and self-knowledge. Do you ever feel like you don't know which way to turn, that you're not sure what the right decision is, do you have challenges being assertive or are you afraid of success? On a physical level, do you suffer from migraines, regular headaches, eye trouble or blurry vision? These are third eye issues. (See above for note on diagnosing and treating disease: don't let your chakra work stand in the way of seeing a doctor when you need one).

The **crown chakra** corresponds to your connection to the divine, however you define that

Its color is violet

Its location is at the crown of your head

Its qualities include: the crown chakra opens you to "the heavens," to spirituality however you define that. This is not about any specific religion, it's about that feeling of connectedness like you belong to something greater than yourself. Do you feel alone in the universe, like no one is looking out for you, or that you don't feel that spark of joy from things like walking in a forest or being in a grand and imposing space? Do you sometimes feel self-destructive, or disdainful of others? Do you lack a sense of awe at great things? These are crown chakra issues. Just as your root chakra connects you to the earthy, grounded, physical things of this earth, so your crown chakra is crucial for keeping the flow of energy moving through you. The goal is balance in all things.

So, as you see, the root chakra is the gatekeeper for all your other chakras. The root chakra is the key to making sure all your chakras are balanced and full of energy. Since the chakras inform as much as they do, cleaning out and energizing the root chakra is critical to your well-being.

Don't worry if in reading about the other chakras it sounded like you may have some issues with other chakras as well. First, as I mentioned, doing root chakra work sets all other chakras in motion as well. Also, chakras are not a zero-sum game. Working on one doesn't mean you can't work on others. This energetic and spiritual work is all synergistic: the healthier your root chakra becomes, the more that transfers to other chakras as well.

2. Can you have too much of a good thing? The overactive root chakra

Is there such a thing as having an overactive root chakra? There sure is. Here are some signs of an overactive root chakra:

Are you often angry, sometimes for what feels like no reason?

Are you quick to anger?

Are you overly materialistic?

Are you brand-conscious and eager to "keep up with the Joneses?"

We won't spend too much time on an overactive root chakra for two important reasons:

1. While every experience is valid, the underactive root chakra is far more prevalent in our culture. And, more importantly, the person with the underactive root chakra is far more likely to seek out solutions, perceiving it as more of a "problem" than the person with the overactive root chakra.
2. (And this is the most important one): the solution for an overactive root chakra is just the same as that for an underactive one. That's because "underactive" and "overactive" are shorthand, something of a misnomer for what's going on. We seek balance in all things, and our energy system most of all. The exercises that "open" your root chakra do something closer to balancing it. It's the same reason there's no such thing as too much root chakra work. By giving attention to the base of your being, you send calming and affirming energy throughout your energy system.

So proceed with confidence. What you're doing is sending love and balance to yourself. Trust in yourself, in the earth, and in the work to get you to the perfect balance for you.

3. A note about traditions

The concept of chakras originated in India, but there are similar beliefs around the world, including in many Asian countries, in Tantric Buddhism, as well as in Hermeticism, in the Yoruba orishas, and many native American cultures. Spiritual traditions are rife with the understanding of the subtle body and the energetic body, and many of them hew surprisingly close to the chakra system. And now science is uncovering how all matter is, at its core, energy, so one of these days the Western tradition is going to catch up with what the ancients have known for thousands of years.

I mention this because however you come to this work is the right way for you. Wisdom comes to us with many names and labels. As with cultural traditions that have migrated, grown, evolved, been adopted and incorporated into other modalities, chakra work can merge seamlessly into your larger spiritual framework. Root chakra work can inform spell work if you're a practicing pagan or Wiccan. Root chakra work can ground you closer during traditional religious rituals. Root chakra work can be completely separated from spiritual work, and you can use it strictly to connect you to the flow of abundance you seek. How you find your way to this work is your own. There are no wrong ways. Just your way.

4. How to get the most benefit from this book

Now that you've got an understanding of what the chakras are and how they manifest in your life, the following chapters will be practical. They are filled with what you can do to clear and activate your root chakra, so you can open to wealth, abundance and well-being. They are tried-and-true and come from a long and effective tradition for clearing a lifetime and even an ancestral line full of root chakra blockages.

As with all things spiritual, doing this work can sometimes feel like a lot. We very often ask for big changes, but sometimes forget that big change can feel uncomfortable and even scary. This is not to say anything "bad" will happen as a result of this work, but that you should be specific in what your request and what you tell yourself you're ready to accept into your life. For example, I once took a cleansing bath on a new moon and asked for the universe to clear any obstacles to my highest good and my success. That very day, my boyfriend of two years broke up with me completely out of the blue (ouch!). A few months later, I got a six-figure advance for a two-book deal I made under a different pen name. At first, the two things did not seem related, until I spent some time thinking about how that boyfriend and I had had issues around money. He had always been very cheap (Goddess love him) and had made jokes about how when I "made it big" he'd quit his job so I could support him. Had he and I stayed together, that big a mismatch in our incomes would have become an issue. I might have even tried to keep myself small to feel like I fit with him, or, possibly, even made bad choices like putting his name on the deed to the house I own by myself. (That was another bone of contention between us). I mean, hey, love is crazy, right?

So I asked the Universe to protect me and clear the way, and it did. I just didn't understand completely what it meant when I made the request. Am I sorry it happened? No. I wanted my highest good, and so it was. The growing pains hurt a bit, though. It's not to say that abundance is more important than love, not at all. It's to say that the Universe knew that love should not compromise my abundance and that I needed different love from someone more energetically in tune with me and my trajectory.

So what does this mean for you? I'd recommend taking it slow. If you're like me, you may want to do every exercise in this book all at once, to get my root chakra spanking clean right now, right this very moment! (If you're not like that, congratulations on being far wiser than I have been at times). But the truth is that this is very deep work. It can bring up emotions. It can create big shifts (see story above!). Think about it: your root chakra has gotten in the condition it's in due to years - maybe a lifetime – of hurts and deprivations, of negative reinforcement, of fear, of lack, of setbacks. You may even come from a long line of financial struggle and root chakra imbalances. Like trying to steer a cruise ship in another direction, the trick is small moves over a long trajectory.

Read the book through if you'd like. Pick out exercises that speak to you. Perhaps incorporate one physical root chakra strengthening pose into your morning routine or add one cup of root chakra tea to your afternoon. Sit with that for a week, watch what happens. Maybe even buy a nice, red notebook and track how you're feeling. See if messages come to you about money, ideas for businesses or side hustles, or other such "intuitive pings." Then, when you're feeling strong and good, add another exercise. And so on.

I am not one to prescribe how you seek your spiritual growth. Check-in with yourself and follow your path. If you feel you're ready for fast and massive change, only you can be the judge of that. I recommend a lot of kindness and self-love, a lot of quiet reflection, a lot of gentleness. The results come at your pace, for your highest good.

You're about to embark on a grand adventure, one which can reshape your whole life. No matter where you are in your journey now, you can find your way to abundance, a sense of deep and abiding safety and more love than you may now believe is possible.

Here we go.

5. Color therapy for the root chakra

The two most basic things about the root chakra are its symbol and its color. We've inserted an image of the root chakra symbol at the end of this chapter.

The root chakra's color is ruby red, a dark, vibrant version of the color. I encourage you to search for "root chakra," go to the Images results and print your favorite in full color. Place it where you'll see it regularly. That alone will begin to activate your root chakra on an energetic level.

Using color is one of the easiest ways to begin to cleanse and wake up your root chakra. You can find small ways to incorporate red into your field of vision. Wear a red top or a bracelet with red stones (we cover crystals that activate the root chakra in Chapter 10). Find a beautiful red photo for your computer wallpaper (an opening red flower or even the root chakra symbol). Same for your phone. Print or buy a mainly red poster and put it up in your workspace or your favorite spot at home.

Another option is to use color-therapy glasses. You can use these glasses over your own, or without any other glasses if you don't need corrective lenses. If you've never seen them, check them out online. Just search for "color therapy glasses." They're clear, plastic glasses, and they come in every color of the rainbow. For root chakra work, buy the red ones. Then, commit to wearing them for a set amount of time. Even five minutes a day will do. You've heard of "seeing the world through rose-colored glasses"? Well, you'll be amazed at the magic that happens when you wear the red root chakra glasses. At first, everything looks red. Eventually, your eyes absorb the red energy, and your perception of the world changes. Then, again, when you remove them, all colors look new. It's a great mental and energetic exercise. When I first started clearing my root chakra, I made it a point to wear mine for a half-hour in the morning and a half-hour in the afternoon. Don't wear them while driving or for any work that requires you to be able to discern colors! Take them off if you feel any unpleasant side effects. But for those of us for whom they work, they are a great way to turbocharge your abundance work.

As with all the exercises in this book, the idea is to incorporate the color red into your day-to-day with intentionality. What does that mean? Well, it means that when you put up the picture or change your computer's wallpaper, you think to yourself, "Every day my root chakra gets clearer and I open to the flow of abundance and security." It's a key thing to remember: intention is the real driver behind all change. Which is great news for you! The fact that you've sought out this solution and are learning about it means you're already on your way, so much further along than most. Setting intentions can give you amazing results.

It reminds me of the quote by the German playwright Goethe:

> What you can do, or dream you can, begin it,

> Boldness has genius, power, and magic in it,

So once you've set your intention for your red items, whenever you notice them, feel gratitude that your root chakra is getting clearer and stronger. Don't worry if you sometimes don't notice it... it's natural for us to become accustomed to the things in our environment. This is often a great sign that our subconscious has incorporated the new things in your field of vision, and they're part of your psyche. Just let yourself feel gratitude when you do notice it and don't worry too much if it's been a while since you have.

6. Self talk to strengthen and clear your root chakra

I've often said it after a lifetime of studying both wealth and the lack of it, and of being poor and being well-off, that the main work one needs to do to "make it" financially is mental. When we don't have everything we want, we tend to focus on the work required to get more money: maybe that next job, or that business we want to start but never seem to, or that extra certification or degree.

But, here's the thing: before any of those things happen, you first need to *believe* they can. And that is way harder than the mechanics of making it big.

It sounds like new-agey mumbo-jumbo, some kind of scam that makes you think you just have to think things and they'll show up. That is not what I mean. What I mean is that we only go for the things we think are within our reach. Would you start training for the Olympics now? Or decide to become a Hollywood actor? Maybe, but probably not. We know what we think is possible, and what we think is out of our reach.

And, truth be told, there *are* things out of our reach. I think personal development books do us a disservice when they tell us "anything is possible." More is possible than we imagine, but some things are *not* possible. For example, unless you started training seriously in the field of gymnastics or figure skating when your age was in the single digits, and unless you're still in your teens, an Olympic dream in that field is probably out of your reach. If you hate public speaking, a career as a self-help guru is probably not your best bet. These are facts and being well-grounded in the facts is empowering. This is not about being down on yourself or not believing in your dreams.

Those facts of life out of the way, the truth is that each of us is capable of so much more than we believe we are. Wherever you are today, if your goal is to become a millionaire, that is an achievable goal within your lifetime. And I mean *wherever* you are. If you're reading a copy of this book you found on a bench you're sleeping on, it applies to you too. If your goal is to write books, even if you've tried and failed a dozen times before, that is an achievable goal. If your goal is to leave a day job that drains you and start a small business that delights and energizes you doing something you love, that is an achievable goal.

But before we reach for any dream, the hardest part is believing it's possible. Despite the previous setbacks. Despite how much money we owe, or how much we're living paycheck to paycheck.

If other people can start a side hustle and turn it into an escape from the day job they hate, why not you?

If other people can travel around the world for a year, why not you?

If other people can make a huge career transition that everyone tells them is impossible, why not you?

I'll tell you why not: before any of those people took the first step, they told themselves, "Yeah, you know what? I think I can figure out how to make that happen." It was only after they made this inner decision that they started working on the steps to get there.

That all begins with self-talk.

For the first part of this exercise, all I'm going to ask you is to observe without judgment. This is harder to do than it sounds! The next time you think of your dream – that big vacation that feels out of reach right now, or that novel you keep meaning to start – listen for what you say to yourself right after that.

If you're like most people, you'll observe that you think things like, "Oh, keep dreaming. No one who does what you do for a living gets to take a vacation like that." Or, "Ha, the old novel thing again? How many times have you bought a notebook and promised to start writing down ideas only to do nothing with it? Face it, you're a procrastinator and a poser. You'll never be a writer."

You know the thoughts. You've been hearing them all your life... from you. Heck, if anyone else talked to us the way we talk to ourselves, we'd probably tell them off. But because we're used to all the negative self-talk – pessimistic messages we absorbed way before we were old enough to protect ourselves from them, usually, from people whose intention it was to keep us safe by not having us stick our necks out and get disappointed – we don't even notice it anymore. The first step is noticing.

Once you notice it, then you have power. As I said, the trick is not to perpetuate the negativity by piling more negativity on top of it. So, when you notice that you're thinking self-defeating things, don't think, "Oh, you're so negative!" Negativity does not chase away negativity. Only love breeds love. Self-love comes from acceptance, and that includes acceptance of the parts of yourself that don't serve you well anymore. Yes, maybe you once felt you needed those messages that kept you from going for things because that meant safety. But it was an illusion. True safety comes from knowing that no matter what you go for, you'll be okay. You'll figure it out.

What does this have to do with your root chakra? All abundance, all enterprise, all the chances you're willing to take, they all flow through a glowing, lively, healthy root chakra. So anytime you catch yourself engaging in negative self-talk, say to yourself, "Thank you for your attempts to keep me safe. I now open to all abundance, knowing that I'm safe, supported, and always figure out the best course of action." It may feel hard, or not so true, at the start. Keep at it. Changing self-talk takes some time, and it's a practice. Be patient and gentle, and you'll be amazed by the results.

7. Affirmations for the root chakra

Affirmations are a simple and beautiful gift you can give to yourself. They are an extension of the principles we talked about in the previous chapter on self-talk. Affirmations are a more ritualized and prescribed way of talking to yourself. If you've been on a path of self-improvement for any length of time, you've heard of affirmations. And, here's why: they work! The mind cannot easily distinguish between what we tell ourselves and objective reality.

Does this mean you should live in a fantasy world? No, of course not. But, like we've talked about before, we only achieve what we first believe is possible. Affirmations are about opening up and expanding what's possible.

What follows is a selection of affirmations for the root chakra. You can work with these however makes the most sense to you. You can choose one a day and recite it to yourself ten times. You can pick ten a day and use them. If you find one or two that resonate with you, choose those and work with them until they really feel like a part of you, a day, a week, a month. Then move on to another one that moves you.

You won't notice the difference all at once. The crazy thing is that you probably won't notice a difference at all. Then, one day, you'll be confronted with a situation you've been in a rut about for a long time (a thing you "can't afford," for example) and seemingly out of nowhere your mind will say the phrase back to you, like "I get to have what I want. I can plan for big expenses if they mean enough to me." And that's when you'll know the affirmations have worked.

Here is a small but telling thing that happened to me, way early in my experience with affirmations. I am terrible at remembering things, so I set a timer for everything. Put a pot of tea on the stove? Timer. Stick something in the oven? Timer. Have to leave at a certain time to meet a friend? Timer. Otherwise time just flies by and I don't notice until the teapot is on fire.

But, here's the thing: I would set the kitchen timer, then walk over to the living room. When the timer would go off, my first reaction would be annoyance. *Do I have to go back to the kitchen already? I'm in the middle of something.* It was silly, but it caused me a low-level irritation every single time.

Then it occurred to me that it wasn't serving my mood to get annoyed at a tool I was using for my own good. I wondered what I could say to myself instead of, "Ugh, timer." I settled on a simple statement of gratitude. "Thank you for helping keep me safe." Or "Thank you for helping me be on time."

I resolved to say this to myself every single time the timer went off. I can't tell you how annoying I found it at first. Being thankful to this dumb, intrusive sound felt totally fake. But I knew I didn't want to be annoyed several times a day. Every little shift in mood counts, and I wanted to live a life of gratitude. Sometimes I'd forget. Sometimes I would find it especially irritating. But I stuck with it.

Months passed by. I went to turn off a pot of tea, and I was struck with a great feeling of peace and abundance. What was it? All at once I knew what it was: I was no longer forcing myself to consciously thank the timer. The gratitude for its very real service in my life had been absorbed into my subconscious. I now *felt* grateful for the timer. I couldn't tell you when it happened. One day, months after I began my exercise, I noticed it.

I have since used that same technique over and over to shift my thinking on many things, large and small. Affirmations work on that same principle. It may feel stilted or even fake at the start. But commit to it. You may be surprised at the great results you'll see.

As you read these, see how each of them make you feel. You don't have to love every single one. It's okay if some don't resonate with you at all. This is just a list from which to choose. You may also find that some seem repetitive. They each have a slightly different construction that work on different levels for different people. See which ones work for you. Write down the ones that speak to you. Say them softly to yourself.

Root Chakra Affirmations to try:

It feels exciting to share my good fortune.

I am safe and secure.

I am worthy of good things.

I am worthy of all I desire.

The universe guides me to safety.

I am divinely protected.

I am safe, secure and protected at all times.

Feeling safe is my birthright.

My family and home are safe and protected.

The spirits that watch over me protect me and keep me safe.

Guardian angels carry me in peace and love every moment.

Anywhere I go I am safe and secure.

I love the child inside me and blanket her with protection and safety.

I deserve safety, security, respect and good things.

The world is a safe place.

All is well in my world. Everything is working out for my highest good.

I am divinely guided and protected at all times.

Whatever I need to know is revealed to me at exactly the right time.

I am loved, and I am at peace.

Everyone I encounter today has my best interests at heart.

I am healthy, whole, and complete.

I am greeted by love everywhere I go.

I am bathed in courage and strength.

I am pure life-force in this physical plane.

I am grateful I've chosen to have this human experience.

I approach challenges with curiosity and trust. All the ideas are waiting for me and I know I find solutions at the perfect moment.

I always find surprisingly good solutions and my ability to conquer my challenges is limitless; my potential to succeed is infinite.

I am an open channel for creative ideas

I am proud of my unique essence. I am the only person on this planet with my fingerprints, my DNA, my life experiences. I am me. There is only one me.

The more good that flows to me, the more I can help others in a ceaseless flow of abundance.

There is enough for everyone. The more I give, the more I get.

Writing your own affirmations

Writing your own affirmations can be immensely powerful. There are universal themes, which the above affirmations address. But speaking to the personal issues you confront can bring this work even deeper. Using the above affirmations as a guide, take a moment to think about the things that make you feel unsafe or like there's not enough to go around. A few questions to get you started:

1. When you worry about the "worst possible thing" that can happen, what does that look like? Is it homelessness? Is it disconnection from family? Is it job loss? Something else?
2. What gets you up in a panic in the middle of the night?
3. How do you feel that are you not enough?
4. What do you most try to hide from others?
5. When you have a nagging suspicion that something is bigger than you are, what is that thing? Or who is that person?
6. When you fear you won't accomplish something really important to you (a lifelong love, a career goal), why do you think that might be?

Take as long as you need. This exercise alone can turn into a powerful journaling exercise you come to again and again. When you're anxious, get into the habit of really delving deep into the reasons with these questions. Every anxious moment, every deep, dark fear reveals a tiny gem, the essence of what it's going to take to heal that part of yourself. Every time you heal a bit of fear, you strengthen your root chakra, and you become more capable of accepting abundance. That's right... accepting. The truth is abundance is all around us. What we need to do is work on our capacity to feel worthy, to receive.

Remember that fear is a tool we use to protect ourselves. The key to overcoming fears is not to push them down but to bring them into the light, to take a look at them, to see what our fears are trying to protect us from. For example, a fear of public speaking might be a way to try to protect ourselves from public ridicule. With that knowledge, you can craft an affirmation to soothe the fear, rather than try to tamp it down.

Once you've identified the fear, find the positive message that you need to soothe it. A few examples using the questions above.

1. When you worry about the "worst possible thing" that can happen, what does that look like? Is it homelessness? Is it a disconnection from family? Is it job loss? Something else?

My "worst possible thing" is not having enough money to pay my mortgage, leading to losing this cozy, safe place I've crafted for me and my family.

An affirmation to address that fear might be, "I am safe in my home, and I easily create revenue streams to give us an abundant life here."

1. What gets you up in a panic in the middle of the night?

My terrible dread in the middle of the night is that I don't know why I'm here. What good am I? What is my purpose?

An affirmation to address this might be, "I open to living fully into my life purpose. I am worthy and important in the circle of life."

1. How do you feel that are you not enough?

I don't do enough. I am lazy. That's why I never achieve anything.

An affirmation to address that: "I trust myself to do the right things at the right times. I deserve rest and recreation."

1. What do you most try to hide from others?

People think I'm so nice, but if they only knew the ugly thoughts that sometimes run through my mind, everyone would hate me.

An affirmation for this might look like: "I accept all of my thoughts as teachers."

1. When you have a nagging suspicion that something is bigger than you are, what is that thing? Or who is that person?

I will never be as good a writer as J.K. Rowling.

An affirmation for a fear like that might be: "I am grateful for my own unique path to the life I want."

1. When you fear you won't accomplish something really important to you (a lifelong love, a career goal), why do you think that might be?

I will never find a man who loves me like my best friend's husband loves her.

An affirmation for a fear similar to this could be, "I trust the Universe (or God, if you're of that type of faith or fate, if you're not) gives me exactly what I need for my highest good in all moments."

If this process stumps you, try to imagine what your most beloved mentor might say if you approached him or her with your fears. Or picture a child you love, one of your own children, or, if you're childless, picture you at your most vulnerable and sweetest when you were small. If that child approached you with that worry, what would you say to soothe them?

This can be an affirming, healing practice you come back to again and again. You don't need to get it right once and forget about it. Fears are natural teachers if we just take the time to listen. Slow it down, stare into the heart of your fears, and you will uncover healing that can transform your life.

8. Sound therapy for the root chakra

Sound therapy is great for working through root chakra blockages because it's another tool you can set in your environment and allow you to work effortlessly as you go about your day. If you like music, sound therapy for your root chakra may be one of your favorite chakra-clearing methods.

We're lucky to live in the age of the internet, because right now, as we speak, you have a complete and exhaustive free library of root chakra clearing music at your disposal just a search engine away. It's as simple as searching for "root chakra music." YouTube, in particular, has fantastic options available, some hours long, which you can "set and forget" in the background. Although they're videos, you can use them as audio and play them in the background. For a somewhat more intense experience, you can also watch the video, which very often includes red images and the root chakra symbol. This can help but isn't necessary. You can also try Spotify or another music-streaming service.

If you don't want to listen to root-chakra-specific music, anything with deep bass works well. Some people swear by Tibetan throat singing. Some people love good, lively drumming. Honestly, anything that gets you up and dancing is working on your root chakra as well. The root chakra is about physicality, about how alive and well we feel in our bodies, so all movement is great for the root chakra. We'll cover this in more depth in the chapter on physical exercises you can do to awaken your root chakra, but it bears stating here: don't work too hard to find the "right" music or root chakra therapy. Have fun, feel alive, and it will begin to take care of itself.

The seed sound of the root chakra

That said, it is notable that each chakra is said to have its own seed sound. The seed sound of the root chakra is "Lam." It's somewhere between the first half of "llama," and "alum" without the "a." If you're wondering how that sounds, again, search for a video. Once you've got the pronunciation down, you can get into the habit of chanting "Lam." This is a good exercise to do while you drive, or early in the morning in the shower. As you chant it, imagine a red light glowing brighter and brighter in the area at the base of your spine, extending out all around you, healthy, vibrant, bright, beautiful. Some people choose to get a beaded necklace called a mala, which has 108 beads, and hold one bead at a time while they chant "lam" 108 times. (Don't do this while driving, though). It's one way to do it but find what works for you. Even ten "lams" in the shower each morning will do the work of clearing your root chakra.

Lastly, some people like using tuning forks, with their clear, resonant and strong vibrations. If you choose to get a tuning fork, the note for the root chakra is "C." This applies to singing bowls as well, another good option.

Sound is an effective, harmonious, and beautiful way to begin to strengthen and clear your root chakra. Try a few of these modalities and watch what happens. Take notes. If you begin to feel more optimistic, freer, and start to have ideas for ways to follow your dreams, keep incorporating root chakra sounds into your work.

9. Herb and food therapy for the root chakra

The root chakra is about being connected to the Earth, to the sustenance that makes us feel whole and alive. So it stands to reason that herbs are a great way to heal and liven up a sluggish root chakra. You can eat them or use them as teas. Some people even swear by boiling root-chakra strengthening herbs and pouring a cup in your bath. As with anything you put in or on your body, if you're pregnant, nursing, take any medication or have any medical condition, check with your doctor. Even after you've done that, you may also want to start slow to make sure it agrees with you.

Because the root chakra is about being connected to the earth, it stands to reason that the herbs and foods that best wake up your root chakra are roots. In addition to roots, red foods (red being the color of the root chakra) are also associated with a healthy root chakra. Here are some of the top ones to choose from:

Burdock: if you are near an Asian market, or a health food store, check out burdock root. Burdock is a member of the thistle family and has a large, slightly bitter taproot. Due to its deep roots, herbalists and wise women throughout history have considered it an herb that grounds you during adversity. In ancient times, it was believed that a burdock root hung from a south door had the power to protect a home from evil. If you can't find it at your local supermarket, the easiest way to consume burdock root may be to buy it dried in tea form. It can be an acquired taste, so you may want to mellow it out with some honey.

Carrot: for similar reasons to burdock, carrot is a great root chakra stimulating root. Its color is bright, and it draws energy up from the earth. Add carrots to your midday meal, or blend them into juice.

Ginger: a beloved spice in cultures worldwide, ginger has an ancient history. Wise women and witches believed ginger is a root that "spices things up," (similar to cinnamon), and probably due to its spiciness, it is believed to be an herb of fire. Because it is a root, and because of its power to "speed things up," ginger is a good root to try when opening up your root chakra. The tea is reputed to help with digestive issues, or you can incorporate its spicy goodness into a stir fry.

Potatoes and sweet potatoes: as with roots listed above, potatoes and sweet potatoes are a good addition if you're looking to work on your root chakra. What's best, if you're cooking for more than yourself, usually no one will think you're adding anything "weird" or unusual.

Beets: these fit the bill in two categories: they're roots, and they're red. Roasted, they make a nice side dish. Beware that if you eat a lot of beets, the red comes out the other end. This can be alarming! So introduce them into your diet slowly.

Turmeric: this root has been growing in popularity since it's been touted as an anti-inflammatory. As a root, it also aids in opening up your root chakra. Boil up the sliced root as a tea and mix with ginger.

Pomegranates: one of the crystals that will be mentioned in the next chapter is the garnet, that ruby red stone with a long history of being used in jewelry. The garnet gets its name from the Latin "granatum," which means pomegranate. If you've never eaten these ruby beauties, you should give one a try. It's something of a meditation to get all the small, red, juicy seeds out of its many nooks and crannies, but their taste is the reward. A healing, energizing root chakra fruit.

Ashwangandha: known as an "adaptogenic" herb, ashwangandha offers benefits such as stress reduction and the relief of anxiety and depression. It also is deeply grounding and strengthening, and a great addition to any root chakra-opening regimen. I like the tea. You can also buy it in capsules.

Chicory root: healers and witches have long used chicory as a "block-busting" herb. Need to break through what's in your way? Chicory is for you. Some people also like the tea as an alternative to coffee. It's a powerful root chakra cleanser.

Dandelion: the innocuous yellow flowers that insist on growing on lawns may mostly be seen as a weed to be gotten rid of these days, but this is a powerful and useful plant. The very thing that makes it hard to get rid of in lawns – those sturdy roots – is what makes this plant a strong root chakra-supporting herb. Roasted dandelion tea is also sometimes used as an alternative to coffee. It's also reputed to be good for the liver and is included in many "liver support" herbal formulas.

ESSENTIAL OILS FOR the root chakra:

In addition to herbs you can ingest as food and teas, other root-chakra-supporting blends work well in essential oils. Do not ingest essential oils! You can use them to dress candles, or in a diffuser. Some people like to put them on pulse points, but test a small patch first to make sure that you don't have an allergic reaction. You can also consult Robert Tisserand and Rodney Young's *Essential Oil Safety* to read up on these essential oils.

Vetiver: earthy and derived from the root of the plant, vetiver is the quintessential root chakra essential oil, and any "root chakra essential oil blend" you find is almost sure to include it. The smell takes some getting used to, in my opinion, so start small. Dab a drop or two on a cotton ball and whiff it while doing your "lam" chant (see the "Sounds Therapy" chapter).

Clove: an old-timey medicine for toothaches, clove oil is strong and pungent and, as its old use suggests, can be numbing. The herb can also call to mind the holidays, as clove is sometimes a recipe in pies and mulled wines. Clove oil is a great root chakra essential oil.

Oakmoss: this deep and earthy scent can feel like a walk in a forest. It has a slightly masculine aroma and can feel deeply stilling. Use a dab to dress a candle or in a diffuser to bring the smell of the forest into your living space.

Cedar: another essential oil that calls to mind a walk in the forest, cedar can be used in combination with oakmoss when creating a root-chakra-boosting essential oil blend.

Spikenard: in the Middle Ages, spikenard was reputed to be a love herb. The essential oil is steam distilled from the root of the plant and its scent bears that out: woodsy and earthy. It can be combined with Vetiver to deepen the effect of both.

Many people prefer a multi-pronged approach to healing the root chakra. Scent and food are a great, sustainable addition to your efforts. It's easy to turn on a diffuser with a root-chakra blend of essential oils or brew up a cup of tea, and the cumulative effects can be remarkable. Giving your body the building blocks to restore itself to balance is one of the best things you can do for yourself.

10. Crystal therapy for the root chakra

One of the most powerful things you can do to cleanse your root chakra is to use crystals. There are specific crystals that are very grounding and powerful in this work. But even just sitting on a rock outside has an effect. After all, the root chakra is about opening up to our connection to the earth, and how much more connected to the earth can we be than to be touching it? Rocks and crystals are millions of years old and contain the wisdom and peace of the ages.

The root chakra is about your sense of survival. Enlisting objects that have been in existence for millions of years can give great perspective and power to your work.

The two general color families of stones that are good for root chakra work are stones that are black and those that are red. There's more to it than color, of course. (Smoky quartz, for example, is neither black nor red but is a good stone for root chakra work). It's more about the stones' energy, a grounding, strengthening energy that certain stones possess.

Using crystals in your work can be as simple as carrying one in your pocket or setting one on your desk as you work (with intention, as in all things). At the end of this chapter, I'll suggest a few other ways that you can set crystals to work for you.

Here are the top crystals to use for your root chakra work.

Black tourmaline: its main function is as a grounding stone, hence black tourmaline's power as a root chakra stabilizer. But black tourmaline does much more than that. It cleanses and purifies. It is revered as a protection stone, doing a great job of deflecting and dissipating negative energy. Because it works on the root chakra, black tourmaline does a great job of opening one up to possibilities and dissipating negative thoughts. A staple of root chakra work.

Obsidian: another black stone, obsidian is born in flames, literally the product of lava cooling. Its glass-like appearance is beautiful, and its energy is not just grounding, but also clearing. Some people consider obsidian something of a psychic vacuum cleaner.

Onyx: another beautiful black stone, onyx has a long history of being used in jewelry. It has also been used in scrying (a type of divination) and is referenced in ancient texts, including the Bible. It is a stone of integrating dualities, not of denying the dark side, but incorporating it in a true understanding of the "yin and yang" of things, that both light and dark are contained in everything. (Many pieces of onyx have streaks of white). Due to this, it is a centering stone and powerful in root chakra use.

Hematite: a stone high in iron, it has a long history of use dating back to the ancient Greeks, who ground it up and mixed it with water to make a red pigment. Its iron content is believed to contribute to its ability to absorb difficult emotions and help stabilize you back to a feeling of groundedness. This stone is believed to absorb anxiety and worry and connect you back to your true, abundant nature. One of the premier root chakra activators.

On to the red stones:

Red jasper: long revered as a stone of endurance, red jasper used to be the stone of choice to give strength to the pregnant woman. Reputed to be a stone of protection, it energizes the sexual organs and the root chakra. It is a stone that is said to bring courage (Siegfried the dragon slayer supposedly had a sword with a hilt inlaid with red jasper). Likely its ability to impart courage has to do with the effect it has on the root chakra, which, in turn, brings a sense of safety and ability to handle whatever comes our way.

Carnelian: the very name of the stone derives from the Latin word meaning "flesh." (Think: carnal). Since the root chakra rules our connection to the physical – to flesh – so the stone named for connection energizes, renews and revitalizes. A stone that helps with feeling "in the moment," it can help unleash creativity and positivity. As such, it energizes the root chakra and lets energy flow through to all the other chakras.

Bloodstone: the name of this stone can feel counterintuitive, as it is often mostly a rich, dark green. However, a good piece of bloodstone is speckled with red. Bloodstone increases the circulation of energy through the body and is considered a true abundance crystal, opening up our energy to receive abundance, and to ease the stress that energy rebalancing can sometimes bring.

Garnet: a beautiful, romantic stone, garnet is almost purely the color of the root chakra. It is a stone that increases passion, a sign of an active and well-functioning root chakra. Garnet lets in all earthly pleasure. It opens us up to being fully engaged in the physical plane, using our creativity and drive for pursuits here on Earth (rather than being "in our heads"). I mentioned earlier that this stone derives its name from the Greek word for "pomegranate," and this stone can often match the juicy red seeds of that fruit.

How to use crystals in your root chakra work

Now that we've identified some of the most potent root chakra stones, what are some ways you can incorporate them into your efforts to bring abundance and stability into your life by strengthening your root chakra?

As I said at the start of this chapter, the simplest way is to get one and carry it around in a pocket. When you first obtain the stone, consecrate it to your work by getting still, holding it to your lips and asking for what you want it to do. It can be as simple as "please work to cleanse my root chakra." Or it can be more elaborate, like, "I open to allowing my root chakra to open and glow, putting me in tune with the energy of the earth and opening me up to the stream of abundance which is my birthright." Once that's done, don't worry too much about focusing on what the stone is doing. Just carry it with you or put it where you work.

One note: I like to place my stones on selenite plates. Selenite is a white stone that cleanses other stones. Since root chakra-cleansing stones can absorb a lot of negativity, they'll work best when they're cleansed regularly. If you don't have a selenite plate, other cleansing methods include washing them in saltwater or leaving them out on a windowsill (or outside, if you've got a private outdoor space) on the night of the full moon. As with all things, intention does much of the work, so as you place the stone on the selenite plate (or in the saltwater, or out in the moonlight), get quiet and say or think something along the lines of, "In gratitude, I ask you be cleansed of all negativity and anything else that doesn't serve."

I like the synergistic effect of using more than one type of root chakra stone together, but even just one, carried steadily, can have an effect. If you're ready for something a bit more intense, get a small red bag (you can make one from a square cut out of an old red T-shirt, or order a fancier red velvet one online for just a few dollars). Cleanse your root chakra crystals as described above, and place with into your small red bag with intention. You can make a ritual out of this, or just simply state your intention as you put the stones in the bag, something like what's suggested in the paragraph above. You can even add a pinch of one of the root chakra herbs mentioned in the "Herb and food therapy for the root chakra" chapter. A sprinkle of dried ginger or a couple of whole cloves works well. Carry this bag in your pocket or purse (the closer it is to your root chakra, the faster and more profoundly it works).

Crystal grid for the root chakra

A powerful way to work with crystals is to use crystal grids. A crystal grid uses sacred geometry to increase the synergy between and the power of each crystal. As each crystal has its vibration and cleansing property, in a crystal grid the strength and use of each crystal are increased exponentially.

Creating a crystal grid can be as simple as putting a hematite in each corner of your bedroom. Or it can be significantly more involved. I have one prosperity grid which includes a sacred design of over fifty stones. I have a special octagonal tray in which I arrange the stones. At the center of the crystal grid, I place jars and candles I use in spellwork to charge them and magnify their work. The effect of this crystal grid is truly amazing.

On this book's Resources page, which you can find at www.AbundanceWitchery.com/RootChakraSolution[1], you will see several recommendations for advanced crystal grid instructions and resources for when you're ready to bust through any blockages in your root chakra. In the following page, you'll also find a simpler crystal grid you can use to start. The silhouette of the person represents where you place the object that needs charging. If that's yourself, sit amidst the crystals as you meditate or do spell work. If, like me, you'd like to use your crystal grids to infuse a magical object with greater power, then use a tabletop or special tray you reserve just for this.

---

1. http://www.AbundanceWitchery.com/RootChakraSolution

11. Meditations, visualizations, and spells for the root chakra

As I alluded to in the previous chapter, there are meditations, visualizations, and spells you can do to strengthen the root chakra. A note about spellwork and why it's grouped here with meditation.

The word "spell" can be off-putting to some people. If that's the case with you, then approach this section mindfully. As I mentioned at the start of this book, you can do root chakra work regardless of your tradition or your spiritual beliefs. Those of us in the earth-based spiritual traditions consider spellwork any ritual, mundane or intricate, which we use to focus our attention and affect the energy around us. Sending out gratitude is a simple kind of abundance spell for people with beliefs like mine because acknowledging abundance puts you in the flow of it. Being grateful for the things we have attracts more things. Like begets like. Sometimes people imagine spells are like in movies, in which sparks fly out of magic wands and things fly in the air. While the results of spells can be absolutely magical, I've yet to see anything fly around. Spells are about focusing energy and stating intentions.

Therefore, when I say "spells," I mean anything you do to shift your energy field, to tune in more abundantly to the bounty all around you. I grouped spells with meditations and visualizations because they all activate a similar state of mind and hone your ability to direct your attention. And, of course, because both achieve results.

I'll start with a meditation. Then, I'll include a few of my most effective visualizations and spells. If spells are not your cup of tea, move ahead to the following chapters, which include other powerful tools for cleansing the root chakra.

In this, as with everything, follow your instincts. If it's intriguing, stick around. If not, pick and choose what works for you.

The Root Chakra Meditation

If you've never meditated, you may believe that you're bad at it. If you're like many people, you think you're bad at meditation because, during the times you've tried, your mind has wandered. Here's the thing though: the wandering of the mind is *part* of the meditation.

Imagine you go to the gym, lift a dumbbell a few times and then give up. As you're walking away, a friend asks, "What's the matter?"

And you answer, "I tried to pick up that weight over there, and it was hard. Every time I picked it up, all I wanted to do was put it back down."

You get the idea. Meditation is about the act of finding your way back to focus when your mind wanders, not about having a mind that never wanders at all. If we all had massive muscles and weights did not tire us out or feel heavy, none of us would need to exercise. If all of us had minds that never wandered, no one would ever need to meditate. But, spoiler alert: no one has that type of mind. Enlightened meditation teachers who can do ten-day silent meditation retreats don't have minds that don't wander. They just have minds that wander less than mine, and probably less than yours. And they got that way through practice.

So, in its essence, meditation is about sitting still and noticing. Not fixing anything. Not chastising yourself when you notice your mind skittered over to the grocery list in your mind again. Just noticing. You can set a timer on your phone (start with a manageable amount of time, like five minutes) and just notice. Some people like to focus on the breath: in, out. When they catch their minds wandering, they go back to the breath. In, out.

For this root chakra variation, the meditation involves sitting cross-legged on the floor, and out on the grass or in nature somewhere, if weather and location permit, and just noticing. Try to keep a straight spine, but don't be too slavishly attached to making it so.

Instead of focusing on your in and out breath, focus on the area where your seated body touches the surface you're on. It's your "sit bones," your perineum... your butt. Extend your notice out to your flanks and to everywhere your body touches a surface.

Notice, just notice. As you know, when you pay attention to a part of your body, very often you feel sensations on that part of your body. You may feel sudden itches. Or maybe a warming, or some other sensation. Just notice. Nothing needs to happen here. This is not a part of your body you necessarily spend a lot of time noticing, so it may feel funny at first. You may feel awkward. It's okay. Just sit still and notice for the amount of time allotted.

The reason this works is that what we focus on expands. Don't worry, I don't mean your butt is going to get bigger! I mean that getting used to feeling the physical area of the root chakra means you are strengthening your ability to direct the energy around it. So, if you can, devote a short amount of time each day to this root chakra meditation. You might even try it in your chair at work (no need to sit cross-legged at that point) or during commercials while you watch T.V. You can try to lengthen the amount of time you do the meditation after the first week. It will help you in all your other root chakra work.

Root chakra visualization # 1 – Earth and Space Visualization

A note about visualizations: it's hard to get quiet and visualize something while having to stop to read a book or your tablet. Audio of meditations and visualizations as a companion to this book is in the works (check www.AbundanceWitchery.com/RootChakraSolution[1], for updates). In the meantime, you're welcome to record yourself reading the instructions below into the voice notes in your phone, then getting quiet and listening to the playback. That does not give you the right to sell it, share it, or in any way benefit from it commercially, but it's okay for your personal use. If you don't have a voice notes app on your phone or get a cringey feeling listening to the playback of your voice (don't worry, happens to the best of us), another alternative is to have a friend read it to you. Then you can return the favor. Whether you record yourself reading it or get a friend or loved one to read it back, be sure to read slowly and clearly. Where it says to picture something, pause and count to five in your mind (or more if that feels right) to give yourself time to conjure the images.

Sit cross-legged if that's comfortable to you. If not, choose the position you prefer. Take a few moments to check in with yourself and see where you're holding tension. One way to do this is to let your head back as if you were pretending to faint. Many of us hold tension in our necks, even our scalps and forehead area. With the high usage of phones, tablets, and laptops, tension around our shoulders and forward hunching is almost epidemic. So just check that area mentally and let go of tension where you can. The trick is not to rain any judgment down on yourself "Why do I spend so much time looking at my phone?" "I should exercise more." This is just about noticing, and then releasing tension. Being kind to yourself is a key component in opening up your root chakra since the root chakra is about feeling safe and supported. Your number one source of support should be you!

The Magic Jewel Visualization

Imagine a ruby red jewel. It's perfectly cut and it's the largest jewel you've ever seen. But this is no ordinary jewel. As you observe it, it glows with a faint luminescence. This jewel carries with it a magic from deep inside the earth, potent, pure, stilling. In its presence, you feel a quiet knowing

---

1. http://www.AbundanceWitchery.com/RootChakraSolution

that the magic this jewel brings is that of peace and security. Stay for a moment in the feeling of this glowing, quietly powerful jewel. However, you experience it is the perfect way. Perhaps you're seeing it very clearly. Or maybe you're just getting a sense of the jewel without a visual of it. Your way is the right way for you.

Now take the jewel from where you observe it and have it slowly make its way to the base of your spine. You imagined the jewel was hard, as jewels are, but as it finds its perfect place at the base of your spine, you feel that it effortlessly becomes part of you without any physical sensation. This doesn't need to make logical sense to be true. The jewel is a glowing, solid part of the earth, and an experience, both at the same time.

The jewel at the base of your spine makes you feel like a gem, and you are. You have this magical, glowing, priceless thing right at the start of you, right at the core of who you are. It has always been there, and the knowledge fills you with wonder and certainty, like it's a story you once heard but had forgotten until right this moment. Of course you have this secret jewel at the core of you. Each of us is a miracle of staggering unlikely proportions. That any of us were created in exactly the way and at exactly the time we were is the unlikeliest of miracles. And so this jewel is at the core of you. Sit with the secret joy of that.

Check in around the area of your root chakra, the base of your spine, and feel any sensations there. Whatever you're feeling is right for you. You may feel a glowing, a warmth, an expansion. Or perhaps you picture this but feel no physical manifestation of it. It's perfect as it is. Just know that you have this glowing jewel, and be with that.

As you sit with the sensation, you notice that this priceless jewel grows in size just a bit. It was already bigger than any jewel you'd ever seen, glowing with life and power. Now it just got a little bigger. The sensation is both thrilling and also like something you knew was a foregone conclusion. The jewel grows and gets brighter, and you sit with the satisfaction of that knowledge.

As the jewel grows, you begin to get an inkling of where it's getting its power. As it takes up a bigger portion of your seat, you can feel the energy, almost like a current, coming up through the Earth and into this priceless jewel at the core of you. It goes through the structure where you sit, to the foundation it's built on, to the earth beneath it. Every stone it passes through, every bit of earth, every living thing, every underwater water table adds its power to the energy feeding your ruby red jewel. You are amazed at the huge amount of energy your jewel commands, and just how much matter and life support it.

The feeling is exquisite, this knowledge that you have unlimited support, that a whole system of living and solid things are working to strengthen and support the jewel at the base of your spine. To support you. You feel a peace and a surge of deep love at just how much power and support you have access to.

The jewel grows yet again. It is brighter, and it opens to further energy. You imagine it or feel it streaming up from the whole planet, up from the deepest reservoirs of magma at the center of the Earth, the parts of our planet that still glow with the energy of birth, raw, fresh, unbounded. The energy binds you electromagnetically to the Earth. You feel the planet spin, and you spin with it. An interesting thing to know about the Earth is that although we think of it going around the sun, we sometimes forget that the sun is moving through space, too, in our ever-expanding universe. So as we move around the sun, the sun moves, which means even when we get to this time next year, we never go back to the place we used to be. We are always in a new place in space, the Earth and us, spinning together, full of power and trust and magic.

The jewel is glowing brightly now. Drink up as much energy as you need. You have a deep knowledge that you can always get your fill. There is always enough. You have so much power and support you can be powerful and supportive for others. This knowledge fills you with peace and gratitude. Sit with this knowledge as long as it feels good.

When you're ready, thank the jewel at the base of your spine, and thank the Earth for its unyielding support. You can leave this visualization with the knowledge that this nourishing, exciting experience is available to you whenever you need it. In fact, it never ends, because your root chakra is always active and connecting you to all that sustains you. Every time you consciously experience it, you strengthen that lifeline. Now, as you thank the earth, add a phrase like, "I now ground this energy so that I may feel balanced, whole and at peace, keeping only the energy I need at this moment."

The reason for this last part, the "grounding," is that when we have very strong energy rushes, sometimes that can make us feel off-balance or overstimulated. The idea is to fill the well, not flood it. So trust that you can accept as much energy as you need in any given moment and that from moment to moment that may change. The more of this energy work you do, the more you will intuitively know how much is right for you in this moment.

It's not unusual to feel euphoric after work like this, or, in the alternative, to feel bone tired, like you need a lot of sleep. Both are natural reactions to the work. Drink a lot of water, eat good, whole foods, and get all the rest your body asks for. You've initiated deep energetic restructuring, and this can feel physically taxing. Above all, be gentle with yourself. You're not being lazy if you need a lot of rest after this. In the alternative, you didn't "do it wrong" if the experience wasn't that strong for you. Trust that it always happens as it should for you.

The strong roots visualization

Begin, as above, making sure to release as much tension as you can. The reason to release tension is that tension, or tightening, can be a blockage for energy. The more relaxed you can get, the more you allow the energy to flow. I sometimes like to take a lavender-scented Epsom salts bath before doing these visualizations. Doing a visualization after a massage or a warm bath can deepen the experience.

This visualization is beautiful if you have access to sitting at the base of a big, old tree. If you don't (if it's cold, or you're in a city without a lot of city parks), just imagining it is fine. But if you want a treat, go find a tree.

First, leave the tree a small gift. A coin will do, or a little slip of paper that says "Thank you," on it. Your experience of your gratitude is what will matter, so let yourself feel grateful for the tree, for all the carbon dioxide it cleans from the atmosphere, for the oxygen it creates, for the home it creates for birds and other creatures, for the shade it gives the earth.

Now sit at the base of the tree. Because trees slope inward and are thicker at the base, you may not be able to line your spine up with the trunk of the tree. That is fine. The idea is to be in some kind of contact with the tree. Sit for a moment, perhaps with your hands on the tops of roots, perhaps with them in your lap. Follow your instincts. Honor the tree as a living being, and check in energetically to see if you're feeling like this is something the tree would also like to participate in. Most trees welcome life coming up to touch them feel listen for signs. Grow still. Imagine what it must be like to live as long as trees live, growing and breathing with the planet, existing in all kinds of weather with pure acceptance. Imagine the power in that, the deep stillness in that. The small joys of being present for birds cracking through their eggs, or of the first really warm day in the springtime. Imagine the experience of a tree. If you're doing this visualization indoors, and not at the foot of a tree, the experience can be much the same. You can envision a really big tree, like a redwood, or a tree you remember enjoying as a child. Or, perhaps, you can envision your tree at an idyllic setting, somewhere you'd love to see, like a great willow by a peaceful stream.

Now that you've settled in by your tree, and spent a little time imagining its experience of the world, take a deep breath and, as you let it out, turn your attention not to the part of the tree you can see, but at everything below the earth that you cannot see. Imagine the tree as the seed from which it grew. Then imagine a tiny leaf first growing out of the earth. How might the world have been different when this happened, fifty or a hundred years ago? What was this spot of land like then? What would the tree have had around it? What was going on in history? Now picture its first, small root shooting downward in direct proportion to the stalk shooting upward. Every tree is different, of course, but imagine the roots growing in proportion to the part of the tree that's visible above ground. See it encountering a small stone, then growing around that. Feel it growing taproots and drinking in the water and nutrients it needed.

Along with your visualization of the trees' roots' growth, imagine your spine growing its own energetic root down into the earth. You understand that this is in complete concert with the tree, not in competition with it, but in gratitude and acknowledgment of its journey. As you breathe in, so too your energetic root grows down into the earth. As you breathe out, you grow more upright and stronger. In, and out, just feel yourself in unison with the tree.

Your root grows thick and strong, a powerful and steady growth down into the Earth. As it does, you feel a pulsating, gently energizing force streaming up from it into you. You may feel oneness with the tree, or you may feel like a distinct being. The tree is your tutor on the simple act of drawing energy from the earth. The more you feel the energy surge toward you, the more gratitude you feel for the tree and its lessons.

You may notice the weather around you, the breeze on your skin, or perhaps any discomfort you feel. Thank it for its lesson and feel confident in your ability to draw energy regardless of any distractions. Your root grows more and more strong and true. Where it encounters obstacles, it finds its way around, just like the tree's root.

As you gather more and more energy, so too do you become a giver of energy as well. You may not be a host for birds on your branches, but you do supportive things for many beings in the world every day. It requires you to have energy, this gift you are to the world. As you feel the energy coming up through your root, so too be confident that you are gathering it so that you can positively impact the world. You are strong, and your strength provides the equivalent of shade for the planet, of refuge for those who need it. Like the tree, you are a hub for making the world a better place.

Stay in this visualization as long as it serves you. As at the end of the last visualization, so too here should you ground the energy you've drawn up so you can leave this experience grounded and relaxed. Also, thank the tree. Put your and on its trunk and speak your gratitude to it. No need to strain to hear an "answer" or worry whether you did it right. Just feel unity with a fellow living being and know that the tree is nourished when creatures (including you!) nestle on its branches and at its base. If you stayed indoors, send out an energetic thanks to trees everywhere for all the labor they do for our planet.

Root chakra spells

Again, as I mentioned above, if you're intrigued by this kind of work, read on. If it's not something you feel like exploring, there's still plenty more for you in the "Affirmations" chapter. While I'd advise that if you're open you might try new things, even if you haven't explored that discipline before, you can still get plenty of benefits if you skip things that aren't speaking to you. This is your journey, and you'll find your way to abundance and a sense of safety in your way.

The Saint John the Conqueror spell:

What you'll need:

- A Saint John the Conqueror root
- A bill (you can buy $2 bills from the U.S. Mint, or even ask for them at your local bank, just for oomph, but any crisp dollar bill will do. If you'd like, you can also use a foreign bill left over from a vacation)
- Red string
- Wealth oil. There are many great options online (you can look at http://www.abundancewitchery.com/product-category/spiritual-oils/ for our recommendations, or just search for "wealth oil" and read reviews of what's available).
- Red velvet or flannel bag (optional)

Sit in your circle, if you're of the circle-casting tradition. If not, you can use one of the visualizations above to get grounded and connected to the earth. When you're ready, rub some of the wealth oil on your palms and roll your Saint John the Conqueror root around, making sure it's well-covered by the oil. As you do, say, "I hereby charge you as a magical talisman to continually strengthen and open my root chakra for my highest good. I open to abundance and I am safe and grounded and healthy." Do this for as long as you feel the energy building, or for as long as it feels good.

Next, wrap the root with the bill, and tie it all up with the red string. Saint John the Conqueror is reputed to add personal power and strength, and it is an effective and continual root chakra opener. Be sure to carry it near your root chakra whenever possible (a back pocket of jeans works well), and add a small drop of the oil to keep it "fed." You can carry it around in a small red velvet or flannel bag, or as is.

Opening the root chakra at the crossroads

The crossroads have long been reputed to be a place of magic, where portals to other possibilities open. As such, it is a natural place to cast a spell to clear your root chakra. What's best, this is a walking spell, so you can use the natural physicality of the root chakra in your favor.

Go on a walk at night. If you've got a root chakra-opening stone, such as a hematite, carry one in your pocket. If not, no worries. Of course, be sure you're in a safe neighborhood! Since one of the main objectives of opening up your root chakra is to increase your sense of safety in the world, this works best in a neighborhood where you feel safe and supported. Pick a corner where you don't normally go, something out of the way to where you normally walk or drive. It doesn't have to be somewhere you've never been, and nothing bad will happen if you pass by it again. It's just that for the energy of this spell, a "new" crossroads works best.

On your walk, be on the lookout for acorns or witches' burrs. If you're concerned you won't find any, it's okay to collect these ahead of time. If you're in a place where these don't naturally fall out of trees, or it's not the right season for it, a pocketful of coins works as well. If you do collect witches' burrs, be sure to bring a small shopping bag to carry them in… these are sharp! Pick them up by the stem.

Now that you've got your offerings, find your way to a four-way intersection, preferably one without too much traffic. (Although if all you've got is intersections with traffic near you, that's fine too! I've done this spell at Times Square with spectacular results). Start at the northernmost corner of the intersection and drop one of your offerings, be it an acorn or coin or witches' burr. Say "I pray, magic of the crossroads, that you help me open to the riches and abundance in this physical world, keeping me and my loved ones safe, and making me part of the flow that nourishes all things." Working "clockwise" (as seen from above), go then to the eastern corner. If the corners don't align this way, start at the northeastern corner, or if you don't know how to figure that out, then just follow your instincts and start where you feel it's best. At the second corner, drop another offering and repeat the request, and do that on all four corners.

Now walk away without looking back, focusing on gratitude and letting go of the outcome of your spell.

Beach spell

Here's a quick incantation you can use while on vacation. Ever wonder why you're so relaxed and happy after a day at the beach? Sure, you're away from all your usual responsibilities and you're having fun. But there's great magical power at the beach, which is why we've been so fascinated by shorelines since time immemorial. The beach is where two powerful elements, water, and earth, meet. Add sunshine (fire) and air (the breeze) and you've got a magical spot.

Salt is a powerful cleanser and standing in saltwater can be a potent root chakra opener. (If you're a swimmer, go ahead and swim, but even if you're not, going in waist-deep is fine. Provided, of course, that you're following the posted rules and the water is safe to go in! Take all the usual beach precautions).

As you stand in the ocean, feel your feet planted in the sand, and the gentle swaying of the water around you. Get relaxed and at peace with the way the water swooshes around. Turn your face up to the sun and allow yourself to feel gratitude for this beautiful day, for your ability to be here, for everything being so perfect in the here and now. It's okay if there are other things away from here that you do need to worry about: for right now, it's okay to let all those go. They'll be there waiting for you when you get back, but right now there's nothing for you to do about them.

When you feel good and relaxed, begin to imagine the ocean water scrubbing away any dark spots or blockages in your root chakra. Ask the ocean for its help in opening up your root chakra. It may prove challenging to imagine the red glow of your root chakra with so many people and all that water around, so if you can't, not to worry. The saltwater can work its magic without your visualization. If you can visualize, picture your red root chakra glowing, sparkling clean.

As with all spells, the power in this simple spell is in your intention. Knowing that saltwater is deeply cleansing, give all your blockages and feelings of lack of safety to the ocean. It can carry them away to where they can be transmuted to something clean and useful in the perfect cycle of life.

12. Candle magic for the root chakra

Candle spells are ideal for root chakra. Although the root is about the element of earth, in the cycle of creation, it is well understood that the element of fire feeds earth. Candle spells harness the power of fire to produce magical results. Candle spells are simple to create and powerful in their outcome.

Since the color of the root chakra is red, a red candle works best. It can be as simple as buying one at your local chain pharmacy in the home goods aisle. What follows are two simple candle spells to activate your root chakra. One truly "bare bones" and one a bit more elaborate.

The so-simple-you-can't-miss root chakra opener spell

What you'll need:

- Red candle
- A slip of paper
- A pen

Get still and allow yourself to feel abundant. This could take ten seconds or it might take ten minutes… stay in a quiet state until you can tap into the feeling of having enough. Perhaps it was at the last family holiday. Maybe it was when you won an award or otherwise felt "seen" for your accomplishments. Maybe it was as simple as the last time you gave yourself a little treat and were happy to know you could spoil yourself that way. Whenever it was, just let yourself relish the feeling. The trick about activating your root chakra is feeling abundant. Abundance begets abundance. So find your way there, no matter how small the feeling seems to you or how disconnected from your larger goals.

Got it? Great. Now take the slip of paper and write the following, "I am safe. I am well. I have all I need." If you feel moved to add other things, go for it. As you'll learn in the section on affirmations, these types of statements work best when they're written in the present tense, like they're already a reality, and when they're positive. So "I have all I need and more" works better than, "I have no more debt." Allow yourself to feel the statement as truth. But how, you might ask? If it's not true, isn't it lying to imagine that it is?

Here's how I like to think of the answer to that: there's an old Native American proverb that says "We do not inherit the world from our ancestors. We borrow it from our children." There is a you, in the future, who knows what it's like to be debt-free. There is a you in the future who is renowned in her field, who has lived everything you wish for and much more. It's up to you to dream her into being. When you state your desires as if they're true today, you're just borrowing that truth from the you you will become. Remember that feeling the truth of something is the first step to achieving it.

Now fold up the paper (folding toward you) in threes. Place the red candle over it on a fire-proof dish. Put your hands around the candle and recite what's on the slip of paper. "I am safe. I am well. I have all I need." Stay in the feeling for as long as feels right. Light the candle.

A second candle spell for the root chakra

What you'll need:

- Red pull-out candle
- Ground cloves
- Dried ginger
- Powdered cinnamon
- Dried rosemary
- Wealth oil

A pull-out candle is a tall pillar in a glass casing. You can buy them at many reputable stores online, including our shop at AbundanceWitchery.com. Once you buy your candle, take it out of the glass casing. Turn it upside down and pull out the wick. Be careful with it, as you'll be putting it back in! It usually slides right out. Using a sturdy knife (and much care!) carve out a small inverted cone at the base of the candle, where you just slid out the wick. Make it at least an inch across in diameter, and about half as deep as a dime. It can be a little bigger than that, but any smaller makes it hard to do the work.

Now slip the wick back in through its hole. Rub the wealth oil between your hands and all over the candle, including the area you carved out of the candle. Take the combination of the ground cloves, ginger, cinnamon, and rosemary and pack it into the area you just carved out of the candle. You can add a bit of the oil to this mixture as well. Still holding the candle upside down, slip the glass casing over it and only then turn it right-side-up. (If you put it right-side-up before it's in the case, you're going to get a shoe covered in herbs).

As with the previous candle spell, the real magic is in your intention. Spend some time holding the candle between your hands and whispering your intentions into it: opening up your root chakra, opening you to abundance and wealth.

Light the candle. Note: never leave a burning candle unattended! If you need to put out the candle when you go out, use a snuffer, or your fingers. Don't blow out the candle, which dissipates its power. Simply re-light it when you'll again be around to supervise it. Loaded candles can do quite a bit of smoking when the flame nears the bottom, so be ready for that. I like to put the base of my glass-encased candles in a dish with water to make sure if the glass cracks the candle is contained.

As always, be safe.

Candle magic is one of my preferred methods of spellcasting. I make my own beeswax candles, infusing them with prayer and intention right from the start. If that's too involved for you, there are many other ways to add power to your candle spells: carve your intentions into the wax itself, poke holes in the candle and load more root-chakra-opening herbs into it, or leave it to charge under a full moon. Making it a habit to burn a root-chakra candle at every full moon will go a long way in your root-chakra-activating work.

13. The physical side of the root chakra

As we talked about way at the start of this book, the root chakra is our fundamental energy center, the way all other energy flows to us. It is also about our physicality: how safe we feel in the world, how at home we feel in our bodies. Very often an underactive root chakra is about "being in our heads," about feeling disconnected from our bodies. It can lead to imbalances in our health, in our digestive system, and our autoimmune system, among other health concerns.

So it stands to reason that physical movement is a great way to get the root chakra moving. One of the easiest things you can do for your root chakra is to go out for a walk. If the walk is in nature, all the better (remember, the root chakra is about connection to Mother Earth, and walks in nature are wonderful for it).

A few other physical things you can do to energize your root chakra:

Drumming. Rock-n-roll drumming could fit the bill, but the best kind of drumming is a more intimate type you do with your hands, like on a djembe. Check out local listings for drumming circles, which can be joyful and fun. But even if you're a solitary drummer, get an inexpensive drum on eBay or Amazon, put on a YouTube video, and drum away. (You can even skip the actual drum and bang on a pot. The point is losing yourself in rhythm). Search for videos on shamanic drumming or djembe drumming. Spotify is good for this as well. Drumming is energizing, it's fun, and it's great for your root chakra.

Squatting. If this is hard for you, don't hurt yourself! But if you can successfully squat, it's a great way to energize your root chakra. When I say "squat," I don't mean squats like you do at the gym. Think of the position you've seen those in traditional cultures taking on when they cook, for example. (If you've never seen this, search for "traditional cultures squatting" and go to the image results. It's fascinating). Be sure not to collapse into the position. Feel your hips widen, but keep your spine straight. Feel yourself drawing energy from the earth. If you feel unstable, you may need to widen your stance a bit. Hold the position as long as is comfortable. Even a few seconds will bring benefits. Create the intention to gradually lengthen the amount of time you can spend in this position. Be careful getting up. As always, be gentle with yourself. You might try combining this with other root-chakra strengthening exercises, like chanting mantras or reciting affirmations.

Yoga. If you're a yoga practitioner, you're already doing plenty to activate your root chakra. Every yoga pose that falls under the "hip opener" category strengthens your root chakra. Here are a few of the best ones:

- **Head to Knee Forward Bend (Janu Sirsasana).** This seated pose gives you a sense of grounding while also developing flexibility in your hamstrings and hips. Sit tall with an elongated spine and your legs stretched out in front of you. Bend your right knee and place the sole of the right foot against your inner left thigh. Rotate your upper body slightly so that it is squared over the left leg. Keep the spine long and the shoulders relaxed. Raise your arms overhead and hinge forward from the hips, folding forward over the left leg. Go down only as far as you can comfortably go with a straight spine. Do the other side.
- **Pigeon Pose (Eka Pada Rajakapotasana).** From all fours, bring your right knee forward toward your right wrist. Imagine sitting cross-legged, but your left leg is extended back behind you. Depending on your body your right knee may be behind your wrist or to the outer or the inner edge of it. Experiment with what feels right for you. The pose should give you a stretch on your outer hip without any discomfort in your knee.

Your right ankle will be somewhere in front of your left hip. Slide your left leg back and point your toes, your heel is pointing up to the ceiling. As you inhale, come onto your fingertips, lengthen your spine, draw your navel in and open your chest. As you exhale, walk your hands forward and lower your upper body towards the floor as much as is comfortable. If you can, rest your forearms and forehead on the mat. Stay for five breaths or longer. As you exhale, imagine your root chakra glowing and opening.
- **Bound Angle Pose (Baddha Konasana).** Sit with your legs straight out in front of you, raising your pelvis on a blanket if you need to. Bend your knees and pull your heels toward your pelvis. Relax your knees out to the sides and press the soles of your feet together. Bring your heels as close to your pelvis as you can without straining. Don't force your knees down. Relax into the pose for five in and out-breaths.

As always, don't embark on an exercise regimen without talking to your doctor. If you haven't done hip openers before (or in a long time) you may find these difficult. Don't push yourself beyond your limits. You're not competing with anyone. The idea is to give yourself the treat of opening up your root chakra without any judgment or injury. As you take these on, gently, imagine you can breathe life force right into the area with each inhalation. This is not anatomically so, but energetically so. Breathe into your hips, and imagine your root chakra glowing red and healthy. Incorporate this into your day as possible.

Kegel exercises. Kegels are everyone's friend! Now there's one more reason to do them: they're great for your root chakra. They're simple and can be done anywhere. I like to practice mine at red (get it? Red!) lights. To do a Kegel, simply contract the muscles you'd use to stop the flow of urine. That's it! They're great for continence and to improve sexual health. So, of course, they're good for your root chakra as well.

Dance. You don't need a dance club or a dancing partner. Put on your favorite music and boogie the night away. Dance like no one is watching (because no one is!). Feeling the pure joy of movement is great for your root chakra.

A final word

You are a magical bit of stardust, an improbable piece of alchemy, spirit made living being. You are a flower, here to bloom, to draw power from your planet, to whom you are exquisitely and intricately aligned. It's no secret that modern living can sometimes make us forget these facts. But you have everything you need right here at your disposal to reconnect with this glorious, abundant, thriving self. The root chakra is a gateway to wellbeing, to hope, to fun, to feeling fully alive. Revisit the practices in this book from time to time. It's okay if you don't try everything at once or if you try something and don't feel anything. This journey is yours. Keep at it in your own unique way. Follow what feels right. Move past what doesn't. You know what to do if you listen to yourself with an open heart and mind.

The road to full self-realization is wonderful, scary, exhilarating, confusing, sublime. It's okay to feel all these things and much more, sometimes all at once. But if there's one thing I want you to take away from this book, it's this: you've got this. You're already so far along on the path. You've just decided to go deeper. The results will be nothing short of magical.

About the Author

Belinda Broome is a practicing witch with decades of study in the metaphysical and spiritual arts. Part of a long tradition, her favorite thing is to distill esoteric concepts into simple and effective solutions. She loves a good hike, has an altar to Hekate, grows as many green things as she can, and finds inspiration in the red rocks of Sedona whenever possible. She's a witchy girl in a serious East Coast town.

www.ingramcontent.com/pod-product-compliance
Lightning Source LLC
Chambersburg PA
CBHW031500040426
42444CB00007B/1159